We the People

THE FIGHTS OVER RIGHTS

Ratification / The Bill of Rights

by Paul J. Deegan

Abdo & Daughters
Minneapolis

Published by Abdo & Daughters, 6537 Cecilia Circle, Bloomington, Minnesota 55435

Library bound edition distributed by Rockbottom Books, Pentagon Tower, P.O. Box 36036, Minneapolis, Minnesota 55435

Library of Congress Number: 87-071091   ISBN: 0-939179-21-0

Cover illustration by Elaine Wadsworth

Consultants:

Phyllis R. Abbott
Ph.D. — University of Wisconsin (Madison)
Professor of History
Mankato State University
Mankato, Minnesota

Bailey W. Blethen
J.D. — University of Minnesota Law School
Partner in law firm of Blethen, Gage & Krause
Mankato, Minnesota

Lewis H. Croce
Ph.D. — University of Maryland
Professor of History
Mankato State University
Mankato, Minnesota

Table of Events

Constitution Signed by 39 Delegates
At Constitutional Convention in Philadelphia   September 17, 1787

Confederation Congress Votes to Send
Constitution To The State Legislatures
(9 States needed for ratification)   September 28, 1787

Delaware Becomes First State to Ratify   December 6, 1787

New Hampshire Becomes Ninth State to Ratify   June 21, 1788

Virginia Ratifies Constitution   June 25, 1788

New York Ratifies Constitution   July 26, 1788

Confederation Congress Sets Dates
For New Government Under Constitution
To Go Into Effect   September 13, 1788

New Government Under Constitution
To Go Into Effect   March 4, 1789

Washington Inaugurated As First President   April 30, 1789

Twelve Amendments Submitted To
The State Legislatures For Ratification   September 25, 1789

North Carolina Ratifies Constitution   November 21, 1789

Rhode Island Ratifies Constitution   May 29, 1790

First 10 Amendments (The Bill Of Rights)
Ratified by ¾ Of The State Legislatures   December 15, 1791

"We the People of the United States . . . establish this CONSTITUTION for the United States of America."

James Madison, the shy, soft-spoken political genius, was on his way to New York City. His Virginia Plan had formed the heart of the new Constitution published in Philadelphia on September 19, 1787.

But this 36-year-old Virginian's work was nowhere near done.

He and others who favored the strong national government called for by the just-written Constitution had a fight on their hands. The fight would be to get the states to approve — ratify — the Constitution.

Technically, the Constitutional Convention, meeting in Philadelphia during the summer of 1787, and the product of that meeting, the Constitution, were only advisory. The existing 13 states would have to ratify the Constitution.

James Madison

Actually, only nine would have to do so. Knowing that ratification or approval probably would be difficult, the framers had not required the okay of all 13 states.

The last and briefest article of the Constitution, Article VII, said the document would be effective if approved by "the conventions of nine states."

The framers did this even though the Articles of Confederation called for amendments to be approved by all 13 states. The Articles were the nation's laws during the Constitutional Convention.

However, before any state could express approval or disapproval — the existing Congress had to act. This Congress was established by the Articles of Confederation. It had to direct the states to begin proceedings to accept or reject the Constitution.

After four months of effort in Philadelphia to produce the Constitution, the framers' goal would not be reached until that document had the force of law. The delegates to the Constitutional Convention who were still in Philadelphia on September 17 had passed a resolution that day.

That resolution said the Constitution should be "laid before" the Congress for the purpose of being "submitted to a convention of delegates" in each state. The resolution said that the delegates to those state conventions should be "chosen in each state by the people thereof."

The wording was not an accident. The framers viewed the chances of approval in many existing state legislatures as slim to none. The Constitution would reduce many of the state's powers. So the framers wanted to increase their chances of the document being approved. They required a special meeting or convention be held. It would have a single purpose, accept or reject the Constitution.

There was nothing in the Constitution asking the Confederation Congress itself to approve the document. And it did not.

However, if a new federal government was to be established under the Constitution, Congress had to send it to the states for approval. That would be Madison's first task in the fight for ratification.

Madison went immediately from Philadelphia to New York where the Confederation Congress met. Madison was a member from Virginia.

Madison prodded his fellow Congressmen. They were hesitant.

For one thing, if the states approved the new Constitution, this Congress would be out of business.

THE FOUNDATION OF AMERICAN GOVERNMENT

Signing the Constitution

Also, Congress included many anti-Federalists, those who opposed a strong national government. They argued that the delegates in Philadelphia had gone way beyond what Congress had instructed them to do. The Constitutional Convention actually had done more than amend the Articles of Confederation; it had thrown them out and written a new national charter.

Some Congressmen were unhappy because the Constitution did not contain a Bill of Rights.

The absence of a Bill of Rights also disturbed others outside of Congress. In fact this was the reason why two of the three delegates in Philadelphia on

September 17 who did not sign the Constitution refused to do so.

Despite the doubts of the Confederate Congress, Madison's quiet persistence paid off. Eleven days after the Constitution had been signed in Philadelphia on September 17, Congress acted. It agreed to submit the new Constitution to ratifying conventions to be called by the 13 state legislatures.

Madison had cleared his first major hurdle. Now the fight over the Constitution began in earnest. Along the way another battle would be fought over the inclusion of a Bill of Rights in the law of the land.

Although Madison and others worked hard for ratification, no one was entirely satisfied with the document written in Philadelphia. The document was a product of many compromises.

Madison, himself, despite his major role in drafting the Constitution, was not entirely pleased. He had written his friend Thomas Jefferson, then in France, that he thought the document which was adopted would not provide a strong enough national government. This had been one of Madison's major goals. However, he ended up compromising some of his ideas in order to get a Constitution written.

Madison wrote Jefferson that he feared the Constitution would not "prevent the local mischiefs which everywhere excite disgusts against the state governments."

The elder statesmen, Benjamin Franklin, had said he did "not entirely approve of the Constitution at present." However, he said, "I am not sure I shall never approve it; for having lived long (he was 81 in 1787), I have experienced many instances of being obliged . . . to change my opinions even on important subjects, which I once thought right, but I found to be otherwise."

Franklin said he signed the Constitution because ". . . I expect no better, and because I am not sure that it is not the best."

Then there was Alexander Hamilton. This foreign-born New Yorker is generally credited as being the one person most responsible for bringing about the Constitutional Convention.

Alexander
Hamilton

However, Hamilton had all kinds of trouble with some of his fellow delegates' ideas. He even left Philadelphia for awhile. However, he returned and signed the Constitution.

He had doubts, however, about the finished product. And, despite his own humble beginning in life, he was no fan of democracy. So why did he become a passionate supporter of ratification?

One historian has said it was a sign of his "remarkable patriotism". Hamilton had made a decision. Under the Constitution, the nation was not going to be governed the way he was convinced it ought to be; but it would be governed as a united nation. That, he decided, was most important.

The anti-Federalists of course disagreed. One of the leaders in New York of the opposition to the Constitution was it's very popular governor. George Clinton, a lawyer, was in the middle of serving 18 straight years as governor of New York.

He would later be Vice-President of the United States and seek nomination as President, only to see Madison nominated, and elected, instead.

Clinton, who was 48 in 1787, was afraid that the new national government proposed by the Constitution would seriously weaken the states. Others felt the same way. Many men believed a state was more important than the union of states or the nation.

This belief was most strongly held in New York and in Massachusetts and Virginia. Opponents of the Constitution were unified and intended to protect what they saw as the advantages of strong, independent state governments and a large population.

Actually, support or opposition to ratification, was to a great extent related to the size of the states. Leading politicians in the above three states were opposed.

Those in small states, such as Connecticut, Delaware, Georgia, and New Jersey generally favored approval. They believed they had more to gain than to lose under the proposed new national charter.

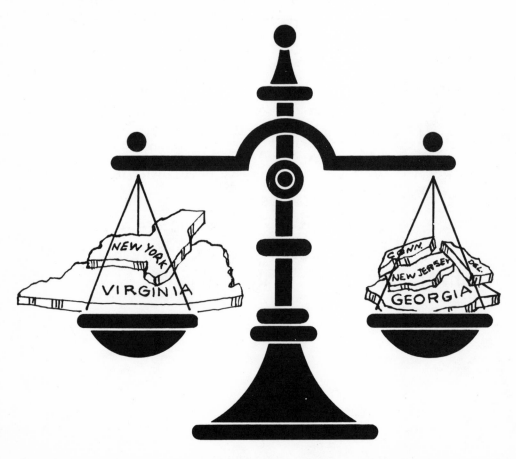

These states quickly set up their special conventions and ratified the Constitution. Delaware did so on December 7, 1787. New Jersey did so on December 18; Georgia on the second day of 1788; Connecticut on the ninth day. Approval was unanimous in Delaware, New Jersey, and Georgia. Connecticut's convention voted 128 to 40 for approval.

Quick approval had also come in Pennsylvania. However, the Federalists, who were concentrated in the Philadelphia area, moved too fast for their opponents. They set up the ratifying convention before the anti-Federalists got organized. The Federalists saw to it that the delegates favored ratification. Approval came quickly by a 46-23 margin. The date was December 12, 1787.

The big battlegrounds were going to be the larger states, New York among them.

There Hamilton turned to the printed word to defend the proposed Constitution. He, Madison, and John Jay, a 41-year-old New York lawyer, wrote a series of essays explaining and praising the Constitution. These essays were published in New York newspapers. There were 85 of them and they are called the *Federalist Papers*.

The first of the *Federalist* essays was written by Hamilton. One story says that the idea came to him while he was on a boat from Albany to New York City.

It is said he wrote the article on the boat. He signed the article with the pen name, "Publius". This was a common first name among the ancient Romans.

The authors of the *Federalist Papers* were writing to the people of New York. The three men wanted the people to convince the delegates to New York's ratifying convention to approve the Constitution.

In that first essay, Hamilton said that "nothing less than the existence of the union (of the 13 states)" was at stake. The "important question", he wrote, was whether a society was "really capable or not of establishing good government from reflection and choice. . ."

Even today, scholars consider the *Federalist Papers* the best explanation of the United States' system of government.

Hamilton is thought to have written 55 of the articles. Madison is credited with writing 26 of them. Jay, one of the nation's Founding Fathers who would become the first chief justice of the Supreme Court, wrote five. The authorship of three essays is undetermined.

Madison's essays included the argument that the new form of government would adapt itself easily to the growth of a new nation.

He also expressed in one of the essays his idea of what the Constitution was designed to do.

"The powers delegated by the proposed Constitution to the federal government are few and defined," Madison wrote. "Those which are to remain in the state governments are numerous and indefinite. The former will be exercised principally on external objects, as war, peace, negotiation and foreign commerce."

The essay also spoke to the role of the states. "The powers reserved to the several states will extend to all objects which, in the ordinary course of affairs, concern the lives, liberties and properties of the people, and the internal order, improvement and prosperity of the states."

However, the writers' arguments were not winning the day in New York.

Ratification by New York was very important. It was possible of course for the Constitution to go into effect without ratification in New York. That was taken care of by the requirement that only nine of the 13 states had to appove. But the new federal government would be off to a very rocky start if a powerful state like New York actually opposed the new system of government.

DATES OF RATIFICATION BY STATES

1787	1788 (Cont.)
Dec. 7 Delaware Dec. 12 Pennsylvania Dec. 18 New Jersey	June 21 New Hampshire June 25 Virginia July 26 New York
1788	**1789**
Jan. 2 Georgia Jan. 9 Connecticut Feb. 6 Massachusetts Apr. 26 Maryland May 23 South Carolina	Nov. 21 North Carolina
	1790
	May 29 Rhode Island

The odds were not good for the Federalists. Governor Clinton controlled two-thirds of the delegates to the ratifying convention. However, the clever Hamilton stalled the proceedings. He successfully maneuvered to have every section of the Constitution examined by the convention before voting. This prevented immediate rejection by the convention.

Meanwhile, skillful maneuvering of a different sort brought about approval of the Constitution in Massachusetts. There John Hancock, the well-known signer of the Declaration of Independence, opposed ratification. But the Federalists forged a compromise built around the promise of adding a Bill of Rights to the Constitution. Massachusetts ratified the Constitution on February 6, 1788. The vote was 187 in favor, 168 against.

Massachusetts was the sixth state to give its approval. Three more states had to do so if the Constitution was to become the new law of the land.

The issue was still being debated in Virginia where Madison had returned home to take on opponents led by Patrick Henry. This was the man who had refused to represent that state at the Constitutional Convention because he "smelled a rat".

The very popular Henry had by then served three terms as governor of Virginia. At the time he was a member of the state legislature and a delegate to the ratifying convention. Henry was suspicious of centralizing power in the federal government. He liked the independent power of the states under the Articles of Confederation.

A Bill of Rights was also a big issue in Virginia. The state constitution had such a provision. It had been adopted in 1776. It was drafted primarily by George Mason, who later refused to sign the Constitution because it did not include a similar bill.

Madison was not excited about amending the document on which he had spent so much thought and time. He had compromised already in Philadelphia. He fought hard to obtain approval without any call for amendments. But he could see that wasn't going to happen.

As he had been in Philadelphia, Madison again became involved in a compromise. He supported a call to the first Congress to meet under the new Constitution to pass a Bill of Rights.

He also convinced a reluctant Edmund Randolph, the Virginia governor from 1786 to 1788, to support ratification. Randolph was one of the three delegates present in Philadelphia on the day the Constitution was signed who had refused to attach their names. He would be the first Attorney General of the United States and later would be Secretary of State.

Madison knew the politics of his state. The same, of course, was true of Hamilton in New York. In Virginia, Madison's skill and work eventually brought him the result he desired.

However, Madison's fight to win approval in his home state took until late June of 1788. Finally, eighty-nine of the delegates to the Virginia ratifying convention voted approval on the 25th of that month. It was a slim victory. There were 79 delegates voting no. The ratification included a demand that a Bill of Rights be presented to Congress right away.

By the time Virginia gave its okay, the Constitution was already the law of the land. Nine states had already ratified the Philadelphia document.

Maryland's delegates had given overwhelming approval, 63 to 11, on April 26. The South Carolina convention ratified the Constitution 149 to 73 on May

23. Then New Hampshire narrowly approved, 57 to 47, on June 21. New Hampshire was the ninth state.

New Hampshire was the 9th state to ratify the Constitution.

Virginia's narrow okay followed four days later.

The New York ratifying convention was still in progress thanks to Hamilton's stalling tactics. However, the anti-Federalists still held an advantage. However, when the news reached the meeting that Virginia had ratified, enough delegates changed their votes to produce a three-vote margin, 30-27, for ratification. That approval came on July 26.

Now, the required number of states had given their approval, but so had the large and therefore important states of Virginia and New York. The 13 former British colonies were going to be the *united* states.

However, opposition to the Constitution was so strong in two states that they had not yet given approval.

Meanwhile, work had begun to set up the new government. The Confederation Congress had named a committee "for putting the said constitution into operation."

The first Congress under the Constitution was chosen in January 1789 and held it's first meeting in New York City on March 4, 1789. However, only 8 of 22 Senators and 13 of 59 Representatives were present. It would be another month before enough legislators were on hand for a quorum so Congress could conduct business.

George Washington was elected the nation's first President and took office on New York on April 30, 1789.

The third of the three branches of the federal government was established when Congress passed the Judiciary Act of 1789 on September 24. This law created a Supreme Court and other federal courts.

The government was in place but North Carolina and Rhode Island, the two holdouts, had still not approved the Constitution.

It took until Novermber 21, 1789, for delegates at North Carolina's ratifying convention to vote 195 to 77 for approval. Their approval was conditional on adopting a Bill of Rights.

Finally, over a year after the new government was in place, Rhode Island's delegates gave their okay on May 29, 1790 — but only by two votes, 34 to 32.

While the national government designed by the framers was being established, the matter of a Bill of Rights continued to be a subject of much discussion. Inclusion of guarantees of specific individual liberties had been a topic of debate from the days of the Constitutional Convention.

During the final week of that convention, the framers soundly rejected a proposal by Virginia's Mason to draft a Bill of Rights. Mason's motion did not get a single vote.

Then, during ratification, Federalists, including Madison, had promised ratifying conventions in several states that if the Constitution was approved, they would see that a Bill of Rights was placed before the first Congress.

By October of 1788, even Madison was more enthusiastic about a Bill of Rights. In a letter to Thomas Jefferson, Madison said he was coming to a point where he could actually support such laws.

Jefferson had worked on his friend, telling him in letters that the people were "entitled" to a Bill of Rights. Jefferson said "no just government should refuse" such a demand.

Madison once had written Jefferson that he thought a guarantee of rights might not do any harm. That was the limit of his enthusiasm for such legislation. He said he didn't see how it could do any good. Madison was responding to Jefferson's first comments on the new Constitution. After saying what he liked, Jefferson had said that what he disliked the most was "the omission of a Bill of Rights."

That bill, he wrote, should provide "clearly . . . for freedom of religion, freedom of the press, protection against standing armies, . . . and trials by jury."

Even today, the freedoms specified in the Bill of Rights — the first 10 Amendments to the Constitution — are probably what Americans like best about their Constitution.

Madison, however, even though he essentially would write the first nine amendments, was not particularly interested in individual liberties or minority rights. In one of the *Federalist Papers*, he made clear that the minority which he wanted to protect was those wealthy persons to whom money was owed. People in general are not likely to take to heart the concerns of this particular minority.

But Madison was a man of his word. Virginia had ratified the Constitution with the understanding that a Bill of Rights would be one of the first orders of business of the new Congress.

Also, if someone was going to make additions to the document in which he already had invested so much, Madison wanted to have a hand in those changes.

However, getting directly involved was going to be more difficult than he might have imagined. His longtime opponent Patrick Henry remained the most powerful man in Virginia politics. The Constitution, now in effect, said state legislatures were to elect a state's two senators. In Virginia that meant Henry would select the first senators. And neither would be named Madison.

Therefore, if Madison wanted to be directly involved in Congress with a Bill of Rights, he would have to get himself elected to the House of Representatives. Madison did not like campaigning for an office. He had hoped for a safe district when the Virginia legislature drew up the House districts.

But Anti-Federalists controlled the Virginia legislature. The district in which Madison would have to run was drawn to try and keep him out of Congress. So Madison hit the campaign trail and told the voters that it was his "sincere opinion that the Constitution ought to be revised (by adding a Bill of Rights)".

That could not have been an easy thing to do for a man who had voted against such a measure in Philadelphia, and who later said he didn't think a Bill of Rights was necessary. In fact Madison had privately described the task of steering such a bill through Congress as a "nauseous project."

However, Madison's campaign was successful. He was elected and went once again to New York City where on June 8, 1789, he proposed to the House of Representatives that they consider amending the Constitution to guarantee some basic rights.

The politicians of 1789 were no strangers to a Bill of Rights. Eight of the 13 states had such guarantees in their constitutions.

Bills of rights define basic rights of citizens' liberties. They also establish safeguards against impulsive violations of citizens' rights by a government.

The first Congress under the Constitution was swamped with proposals for amendments dealing with rights and safeguards. Seventeen of them came from Madison. He used Virginia's Bill of Rights as a model for his proposals.

JAMES MADISON

Nine of Madison's proposals survived in the Bill of Rights in much the same form as he presented them.

The 10th Amendment was the product of Richard Henry Lee, another Founding Father from Virginia. Lee had introduced the resolution in the Second Continental Congress calling for a declaration of independence. Later, he had opposed ratification of the Constitution.

The 10th Amendment was proposed to make clear that states still had powers of their own, a point particularly important to those who feared the strong national government set up by the Constitution.

Given a choice, Madison probably would have given all powers to the federal government. In fact, one amendment Madison did propose would have limited state governments. It would have been the only such amendment in the Bill of Rights.

Madison called this proposal the most valuable amendment in the whole list. It would have required that the states respect freedom of conscience and speech as well as grant jury trials in criminal cases.

The Senate, however, threw it out.

Thus a truth of history often not recognized. Americans today are very proud of the rights guaranteed them by the first 10 amendments. However, many don't realize that most Americans living from 1791 until 1868 had no such protection. The Bill of Rights, which went into effect in 1791, did not apply to the states!

Citizens were protected by the United States Constitution only in their dealings with the federal government.

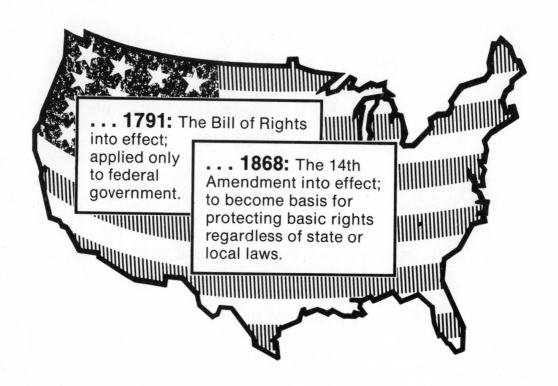

... **1791:** The Bill of Rights into effect; applied only to federal government.

... **1868:** The 14th Amendment into effect; to become basis for protecting basic rights regardless of state or local laws.

States could and did limit basic freedoms, unless forbidden to do so by their own constitutions.

The 14th Amendment, ratified in 1868, gave federal courts an opening to apply the guarantees of basic rights to a person's relationship with state governments. This amendment says "nor shall any state deprive any person of life, liberty, or property without due process of law."

The 14th Amendment, as was the 13 Amendment, were by-products of the Civil War and the consequent ending of slavery in the United States. The reason Congress produced the 14th Amendment in 1866 was to protect the rights of the now free black slaves.

However, in the more than a century since it was ratified, it has been the basis of a long series of Supreme Court decisions.

These court rulings, in effect, now have made the specific protections of the Bill of Rights as effective with regard to states as they were previously with regard to the national government. But this was true for many years generally only if the person was a man or, sometimes, if the person was black.

Some protections in the Bill of Rights were not applied fully to women until court cases decided in the 1970s.

Originally, however, citizens were so protected only in their relationships with the federal government.

Actually, the basic guarantees of rights are in the first eight amendments. The Ninth, as well as the 10th Amendment, concern rights held by the states and the people.

These two amendments were included in the Bill of Rights mostly to calm the fears of the anti-Federalists. These supporters of states' rights were worried that the national government might eventually try to add powers not specifically granted to it under the Constitution.

The first 10 amendments, and two more, were passed by both houses of Congress by September 25, 1789. On October 2 President Washington sent them to the states for ratification or approval.

The Constitution spells out in Article V how it can be amended. An amendment can be proposed by Congress. Two-thirds of both houses have to approve it. Then three-fourths of the states must ratify the proposed amendment before it becomes part of the Constitution.

Article V says an amendment can also be proposed by a convention for that purpose by Congress at the request of two-thirds of the state legislatures. In almost 200 years this has never happened.

With 13 states, the approval of 10 was needed to add the Bill of Rights to the Constitution. Nine states ratified within a short time of receiving the proposals. Virginia stalled. Finally, more than two years after Congress gave its approval, Virginia ratified the 10 amendments and they became effective December 15, 1791.

The two proposed amendments that were never ratified concerned Congress. One related to salary; the other to the number of members from each state.

The amendment with which people are most familiar is the 1st Amendment. It is less than 50 words, but covers some of the gut issues of personal freedom. This amendment says:

"Congress shall make no law respecting an establishment of religion, or prohibiting the free exercise thereof; or abridging the freedom of speech, or or the press, or the right of the people peaceably to assemble, and to petition the government for a redress of grievances."

Madison's viewpoint is very much reflected in the 1st Amendment. He was involved in the passage of a 1786 bill in the Virginia legislature which established religious freedom in that state. He had an appreciation of the danger of permitting one religion to force people to accept it's belief.

One historian has said that "To Madison, more than to any other Founding Father, freedom of religion was the first freedom, the cornerstone of a free society."

His views are said to reflect a couple of things. One was his education at the College of New Jersey (now Princeton University). Another was watching the Anglican church, when it was the state-supported church, persecute Baptists in Virginia.

Basically, the 1st Amendment means that a person can worship — or not worship — as he or she pleases. Congress cannot say everyone must follow a particular religion.

The word "abridging"* in the amendment means to cut short or take away from. Therefore, in terms of "freedom of speech" you can say what you want or listen to what you want even if the subject is not popular. There are some limits. The often used example of limitations is that a person doesn't have the right to shout "fire" in a crowded area when there is no fire.

Freedom as applied to the press meant to the framers that newspapers were not subject to any government control over what they printed. They could criticize the government or a government official without being shut down. The right to do this was established in colonial New York. You cannot knowingly print mistruths.

The freedom to assemble means you can meet as you wish, even to protest if it is peaceable. Freedom to petition means you can ask the government to change something you think is wrong. "Redress" means to set right. "Grievances" are real or imagined causes for protest.

*The definition in this book of a word used in the Bill of Rights is a contemporary literal definition of the word in its context, not the legal meaning of a word, which may have been interpreted, or might be subject to interpretation by, a court or courts of law.

The 2nd Amendment says:

"A well-regulated militia, being necessary to the security of a free state*, the right of the people to keep and bear arms, shall not be infringed."

The 2nd Amendment relates to the way things were at the time. There was no standing army in 1789. There were no state patrols or local police forces as we know them. A "militia" is a citizen army, rather than professional soldiers, that was called to serve in an emergency. "Infringed" means to be violated.

*The first letter of the word "state" or "states" was capitalized in the original Bill of Rights.

The 3rd Amendment was drafted because before independence the British had forced colonists to house British soldiers. It reads:

"No soldier shall, in time of peace be quartered in any house, without the consent of the owner, nor in time of war, but in a manner to be prescribed by law."

"Prescribed" means spelled out or stated.

The fourth through the eighth amendments set out basic guarantees with regard to legal procedure. They reflect long-held principles of British law.

The 4th Amendment limits the authorities' right to search. Most importantly, it forbids *unreasonable searches* although it does not forbid searches. It says:

"The right of the people to be secure in their persons, houses, papers, and effects, against unreasonable searches and seizures, shall not be violated, and no warrants shall issue but upon probable cause, supported by oath or affirmation, and particularly describing the place to be searched, and the persons or things to be seized."

A "warrant" is a court order. "Shall issue" means grant or order (a warrant).

The fifth amendment is the longest of the first ten amendments. It covers several topics.

It says that in most instances someone who commits a serious crime cannot be charged with that crime unless the case is presented to a group of citizens known as a "grand jury."

It says that no one should be tried twice for the same crime. If a person is once found innocent, the government cannot try that person again on the same charges in hopes of getting a conviction on another try.

The person charged with a crime has the right to remain silent and does not have to testify in the trial of his or her criminal case, according to the 5th amendment.

The last part of the amendment says the government must respect the right of private property.

Remember, that when ratified the Bill of Rights related only to the national government, not the states.

The 5th Amendment reads:

"No person shall be held to answer for a capital, or otherwise infamous crime, unless on a presentment or indictment of a grand jury, except in cases arising in the land or naval forces, or in the militia, when in actual service in time of war or public danger; nor shall any person be subject for the same offense to be twice put in jeopardy of life or limb; nor shall be compelled in any criminal case to be a witness against himself, nor be deprived of life, liberty, or property, without due process of law; nor shall private property be taken for public use, without just compensation."

A "capital" crime is one in which the penalty is death. "Infamous" means very bad. A "presentment" is giving a formal legal statement to, usually, a court. An "indictment" is a written statement charging someone with a crime. "Compelled" means forced. "Deprived" means to be taken away. "Compensation" means payment.

The 6th Amendment concerns the rights of a person accused of a crime. It does not deal with civil (non-criminal) cases or trials. What it says is quite clear. It reads:

"In all criminal prosecutions, the accused shall enjoy the right to a speedy and public trial, by an impartial jury of the state and district wherein the crime shall have been committed, which districts shall have been previously ascertained by law, and to be informed of the nature and cause of the accusation; to be confronted with the witnesses against him; to have compulsory process for obtaining witnesses in his favor, and to have the assistance of counsel for his defense."

"Ascertained" means spelled out or defined. The "accusation" is the charge against a person.

"Confronted with the witnesses . . ."means the person charged with the crime, the defendant, has the right to know from whom the government got its information about the crime. "Compulsory" means something is required.

The 7th Amendment guarantees jury trials in certain civil suits. It says:

"In suits at common law, where the value in controversy shall exceed twenty dollars, the right of trial by jury shall be preserved, and no fact tried by a jury, shall be otherwise re-examined in any court of the United States than according to the rules of common law."

Twenty dollars, of course, was seen at the time as a good deal of money. "Common law" is the system of laws which began and was developed in England. It is based on decisions of courts and custom, not written laws.

The 8th Amendment reads:

"Excessive bail shall not be required, nor excessive fines imposed, nor cruel and unusual punishments inflicted."

"Excessive" means more than necessary. "Bail" is something of value, usually money, which an accused person puts up to gain his release. The government keeps the money if the person fails to appear in court.

This amendment talks about "cruel and unusual punishments" because at the time some convicts were actually cut apart or burned at the stake.

The 9th and 10th amendments concern rights held by the people and the states. Both were included to ease the fears of those who feared the powers of a strong national government.

The 9th Amendment says:

"The enumeration in the Constitution of certain rights shall not be construed to deny or disparage others retained by the people."

"Enumeration" means as stated or as explained. "Construed" means read or interpreted. "Disparage" means to make less of or reduce.

The final amendment included in the Bill of Rights, the 10th, leaves to the states any power that has not been given in the Constitution to the national government. It reads:

"The powers not delegated to the United States by the Constitution, nor prohibited by it to the states, are reserved to the states respectively, or to the people."

These 10 amendments were the first changes in the Constitution. Looking back, it was a very important decision the framers made in permitting change. They could not know how different the United States would be 200 years later. But they obviously realized two things.

One, they had not written a perfect document. Two, they could not predict the future.

So they included Article V in the Constitution and gave us an orderly method of change. The foremost law of the land could be modified in order to meet changing needs. But the demand that three-fourths of the states approve has meant any change is difficult to achieve.

Since 1789 over 9,000 amendments to the Constitution have been proposed. Only 16 other than the Bill of Rights have been ratified by the states.

Of the 26 amendments to date, the Bill of Rights are the ones with which Americans are most familiar. They protect something Americans value highly. Writing in the 200th anniversary year of the Constitution, the Supreme Court's first black justice, Thurgood Marshall, reminded us of what they protect. He called them "fundamental human rights."